The Silk Road

by Tony Bradman
illustrated by Emmanuel Cerisier

CAMBRIDGE
UNIVERSITY PRESS

Institute of Education

Chapter 1

A long time ago in China, there lived a boy called Cheng. He was ten when the bandits came and changed his life forever.

They rode out of the hills and burnt down his family's farm. His father yelled, 'Run!' and Cheng did as he was told, but it was too late for his parents.

Cheng hid in the forest and wept for his mother and father. But he knew crying wouldn't bring them back - he would have to look after himself now.

So he set off to find a new home.

He went to the nearest village but nobody there was willing to take him in.

'Times are hard, boy,' said the village elder. 'We barely have enough to feed our own families, so another hungry mouth isn't welcome. You'll have to try somewhere else!'

Cheng heard the same harsh words at the next village, and the next. He grew hungry and tired, and he had never felt so lonely.

Then, one day, he climbed a hill and saw ... the Silk Road.

It stretched from east to west, as far as he could see in both directions.

Cheng's parents had talked about it, of course. Merchants travelled along it, taking Chinese silk to the West. But many other things were traded, too - pearls from Arabia, carpets from Persia, horses, camels, even slaves.

A long line of carts and people and animals was
going by. Cheng looked at them for a while, then
shrugged. 'I've got nothing to lose,' he thought.

He walked down the hill and joined them.

Chapter 2

Nobody on the road took much notice of Cheng, and he was happy with that.

Some of the people were Chinese, but many weren't. They wore strange clothes and spoke strange languages, and a few rode strange animals.

After a while, Cheng saw an inn at the side of the road. A rich man gave Cheng a silver coin to keep an eye on his horse while he went inside.

Cheng spent it on a hot meal.

That night, Cheng slept in the warm straw of the stables behind the inn.

Over the next few days, he earned more silver coins. He kept an eye on the horses of rich men, he carried bags, he cleared tables for the innkeeper.

Eventually, the innkeeper said he could sleep in a store room. 'Just watch out for the rats,' he said. Cheng made his corner as comfortable as he could.

But it didn't feel like home.

Time passed, and Cheng earned his silver coins, but he felt restless.

One day, he got talking to an old man. 'There's more to life than this dirty little inn, you know,' said the old man. 'You can find anything on the Silk Road.'

Perhaps the old man is right, Cheng thought.
It was time to move on. So the very next
morning, he packed a bag, said goodbye to
the innkeeper and set off. He didn't look back.

There were other inns, of course, and more silver coins to be earned. He looked after horses, guarded wagons, spent whole nights watching the goods for the merchants.

But Cheng was also learning about trading. He saw how the best merchants haggled and made deals, so he did the same.

'You want me to keep an eye on your horse?' he said. 'Well, it's one silver coin for the first hour, then two for the next hour …'

'You strike a hard bargain, boy,' the rich merchants replied.

But they always paid, because Cheng always did a good job.

There were other things to be learned on
the Silk Road.

Cheng learned many new languages. Before long,
he could talk to merchants in their own tongues
and making deals became even easier.

He learned something about the lands they came from, too - the deserts and forests, the cities of China, India in the south, Persia and Europe in the west.

It seemed the whole world travelled on the Silk Road.

But most importantly, Cheng learned how to see danger coming.

Bad people of all kinds found their way to the Silk Road. Several times, Cheng saw bandits attacking a caravan, killing the merchants and stealing their wares. He would freeze, willing them not to attack the caravan he was guarding, terrified and alone.

But many of the bad people were more cunning. They were the kind who pretended to make friends with travellers … then robbed them when they got the chance.

Cheng made sure that it never happened to him.

Chapter 3

The days passed, and Cheng survived on the Silk Road, but he wasn't happy.

After a while, he began to think the old man at the first inn had been wrong.

You could find lots of things on the Silk Road, but not a new home.

Cheng got to know many merchants, and they were always pleased to see him. But he usually ended up alone in a barn or a corner somewhere.

He was lonelier than ever.

One day, he came to a place where many people had set up camp.

There was a well with clean water, and everybody seemed friendly. Cheng passed a man and woman sitting by their small horse-drawn wagon.

'Hello there!' said the man, smiling at him. 'Could I offer you something to eat, my friend? My wife and I could do with some good company.'

Cheng smiled back and nodded. He could tell they were good people.

The couple were called Haroun and Amina, and they were very nice.

It turned out they had come all the way from Persia. 'I decided I wanted to be a merchant,' said Haroun. 'I mean, how hard can it be?'

'Too hard for you,' said Amina. 'We're not making much money, are we?'

'But we're seeing the world,' said Haroun, 'and meeting interesting people!'

'Still, it would be nice to have a family one day,' said Amina with a sigh.

Cheng could see she really meant it.

The next day, Cheng went to find Haroun and Amina again.

Three men were sitting at the couple's campfire. Cheng didn't like the look of them, and he tried to warn Haroun. But Haroun just laughed.

'Oh no, they're fine fellows!' he said. 'You worry too much, Cheng!'

Cheng was sure the men were robbers, and he decided he would keep an eye on Haroun and Amina in case something happened. That night, he hid near their wagon.

He didn't have long to wait. Three shadows crept out of the darkness …

'Wake up, Haroun and Amina!' Cheng yelled. The couple leapt to their feet and a fight began. Haroun was strong and brave, and Amina fought them, too.

28

Still, they were about to lose their goods … when Cheng joined in as well! 'Take that!' he yelled as he fought, remembering the bandits who had changed his life forever.

Soon the robbers were defeated, and ran off into the darkness.

Haroun and Amina were so grateful to Cheng that they asked him to travel with them.

'You must stay with us. We will look after you. You are like a son to us!' said Amina.

The old man had been right about the Silk Road. Cheng had found a family and a home at last, even if he never stayed in one place for too long. With Cheng's help, Haroun and Amina soon became pretty good merchants, too.

And Cheng was never lonely again.

The Silk Road · Tony Bradman

Teaching notes written by Sue Bodman and Glen Franklin

Using this book

Developing reading comprehension

This is a story based on historical fact. The events unfold over three short chapters as Cheng leaves his home and makes his way alone in the world. The sophisticated themes will be challenging for some younger, more able readers, but offer an opportunity for older, struggling readers to read a simpler text at a high interest level.

Grammar and sentence structure

- Sentences are longer, with subordinate phrases or clauses.
- Paragraphing and page layout serve to support the meaning and build tension.
- The use of connective words and phrases (such as *'Eventually'* and *'After a while'*) are used to structure the passing of time.

Word meaning and spelling

- New subject-specific vocabulary is introduced (*'merchants'*, *'haggling'*).
- Meaning is monitored and checked through use of dictionaries and contextual information in text.
- Place names, titles and new vocabulary words are read using decoding and word-recognition skills.

Curriculum links

History – Read other accounts of the Silk Road in books or via the Internet sites.

Geography – Trace the route of the Silk Road on a modern map. Find what goods were traded from which countries along the route.

Citizenship – Cheng was lucky to meet with people who helped him along the way. Explore modern-day equivalent stories and biographies of people supporting others in times of trouble.

Learning Outcomes

Children can:

- sustain interest in longer text, returning to it easily after a break
- explore how particular words and phrases are used
- express reasoned opinions about what is read
- monitor meaning and understanding, and take action when meaning is lost.

A guided reading lesson

Book Introduction

This book is written in three chapters. It is possible to use the book over two guided reading lessons, setting Chapter 2 as an independent reading activity in between each lesson.

Give a copy of the book to each child. Ask them to read the title and the blurb independently.

Orientation

Ask the children to tell you of their predictions for this story, based on their reading of the blurb.

Tell them: *This book is written in three chapters. Today we are going to read Chapter 1. In this book, a young boy called Cheng has to leave his home. He goes on a long journey and many things happen to him before he finds a new home. It is a story that happened a long time ago. Where do you think the story is set?*

Preparation

Page 2: *What happened to make Cheng leave his home? Where can you find evidence for that in the text?*

Page 4: *One of the villagers says 'Times are hard, boy'. What does he mean by that?*